MW00886575

# THIS NOTEBOOK BELONGS TO:

••••••••••••••••••••••••••••••••

••••••••••••••••••••••••••••••••

Made in the USA
Monee, IL
04 November 2022

17094114R00057